CRASH ON J BIRD ROAD

The Untold Story of an Unlikely Ally

VAN GRIFFIN

CRASH ON J BIRD ROAD
THE UNTOLD STORY OF AN UNLIKELY ALLY

Copyright © 2014 Van Griffin.

iUniverse books may be ordered through booksellers or by contacting:

iUniverse LLC
1663 Liberty Drive
Bloomington, IN 47403
www.iuniverse.com
1-800-Authors (1-800-288-4677)

ISBN: 978-1-4917-3750-7 (sc)
ISBN: 978-1-4917-3751-4 (e)

Printed in the United States of America.

iUniverse rev. date: 07/09/2014

PRELUDE

What if I told you getting my car stolen twice in the same night was not even in the top three of the craziest moments of my life?

Would you believe me if I told you almost a year to the day of my vehicle's recovery, I was pulled over by what felt like, half of a police force? With guns drawn, I was handcuffed because the police did not properly record my car as being recovered. They recorded the tag but not the VIN (Whatever that means). Do you think that is in my top three? The answer is still no.

What about if I told you I was involved in an accident where the vehicle flipped over 3 times. It landed almost right in front of a hospital. And the driver, who was not wearing a seatbelt, survived only needing forty five stitches. Would that be in my top three maybe? Nope.

I have a story to tell you about an individual who has seen more than his share of drama. That individual is me. And neither of the above stories will be included within these pages because they are not worthy. I have seen enough to write a book about it. And as entertaining as you may find it, it was these events that shaped who I am today, for better or for worse. These events you are going to read about are all true. Some of the names have been changed and some of the dates are a little foggy, but you will get the idea. This is the tale of one man's journey through life and the many experiences that have shaped his views of people, politics and pursuits.

I hope you enjoy.

Chapter 1

WAKE UP CALL

Her name seems to escape me at this time, but I remember the situation very well. It was at least 7 or 8 years ago and I was a recently promoted supervisor at a tech company. I had been working at this place for about 10 months. The company is no longer in our city and I could give you a myriad of reasons why but I digress. Anyways, being in the role of a supervisor you observe many details about the people that report to you. I remember my favorite line, "I can teach you anything you need to know about the job but I can't teach you to be here on time. That is out of my hands." I am laughing at myself right now just thinking about how many times I have uttered those words. Anyway, back to the subject at hand. I had interviewed many people in this position even though I had only been in this role for a couple of months. To give a little insight into the way this business was run, it was a call center. Aside from the managers, supervisors and other support staff, we had a contract with a large internet company to continually have 400 associate staffed and on the

1

phones at any given time. The interviews were usually very quick and to the point. Later on in my life I use to joke around about that job interviewing process. I use to tell how the process would go and it was something like this: I would walk in the room and the potential candidate would be sitting at a small table. Nothing would be in my hand except for a mirror that would fit quite snug in ones pants pocket. I would sit down across from the nervous person who probably had no idea how desperate we were for people. I would not say a word, rather, I would just hold that pocket sized mirror under their nose. If it fogged up, they were hired. I hope you get it. If not ask a friend. My point is barring a jail sentence we would hire just about anybody to keep the phones manned. That is how I got the job in the first place but I will talk about that a little later.

Now that you know a little about the hiring process hopefully you can understand my excitement when a good candidate came along. This particular young lady I mentioned at the beginning of this story was not someone that I hired. She had actually been working at the place years before I even arrived. On one of the many shift changes, she ended up on my team for the next few months. I usually had a team for 2 or 3 months and then the other supervisors and I would switch teams. I think management did that to avoid any complacency from the associates, but I never really cared to ask why.

Let's call this young lady Kate for now. The story is easier for me to tell and probably for you to understand with a name. Kate was just your average black woman in her early twenties. She always stuck out to me because she was tall and always dressed nice like she was going to an office job....a good office job. This job did not pay minimum wage but I would in no way call it a great hourly wage. But she treated it that way and I admired that about her. I was excited to finally have her on my team because the other supervisors that she worked for always gave her great praise. After about the first 2 weeks with my new team I had already fired one person and another one just stopped showing up. It was just another day in the life of a call center. If you have ever worked for one you understand I am sure. One day I pulled one of the other supervisors to the side to ask about Kate. I was curious to know why she had been there so long and never moved up. Even though there were 400 people, a very, very small percentage of the group had potential for upward growth. The answer was not what I was expecting. I was told by this supervisor, "I really have no idea because she is smarter than most of the folks here. And that goes for the managers and supervisors." I chuckled a bit and then got serious with her again. I said, "Seriously have you ever asked her? How long has she been here?" She responded again, "Why would I ask her that? I don't want to get all in her business. I am pretty sure she has been here at least 4 years." I let the conversation go after that. I did not ask anyone else after that because I thought it was a safe assumption I would get the same answer. After about a month had gone by it was time for our "one on ones." This was going to be my chance to learn a little more about this intriguing woman and possibly get a little info into her goals and aspirations. I was not going to be too nosey, but was also not intent on just going over stats for the previous month.

If memory serves me correctly (and it usually does not) I was working the one to ten shift at this time. The internet company that we use to contract for dumped us, and we ended up with a satellite TV company. That company only wanted us to work the late shifts so my team's shift was one o'clock to ten o'clock PM. On a side note, that shift change only made things for the company worse because many of the veterans and good associates could not work nights and the job did not pay them enough to stay and change their daily routine. Some of them had families and some of them were retired and just working there for extra bill money. That is when the company started going downhill even faster but once again that story is for another time. I remember when we were moved to nights I would always make it a point to start my one on ones each month as soon as I showed up for work. I would try to squeeze in at least two or three before the daily drama reached full force. The day that I sat down to do Kate's one on one, she was the first one of the day. I remember this because she was always early as was I and we walked in together that day. "Kate I know it is early but did you want to go ahead and do your one on one before things begin to get crazy?" I asked. "That's fine. I still have 20 minutes before I have to be on the phones." Kate replied. So off Kate and I went to my usual office amongst the many that surrounded the center floor. You see the supervisors did not have offices only the managers did. We sat on the floor with our individual teams. I always wondered why there were so many offices and only 4 managers. Who knows as that was one of many things I did not understand about that job. Anyways, I asked Kate to have a seat and she complied. I then sat down across from her on the other side of the desk. Think about the interview setting I mentioned earlier minus the mirror. The meeting started as most of them normally do. Kate's talk times and all other stats were at or above goal. That actually worked to my advantage because we were able to get past that part pretty quickly. I then ask all of my associates the same question after we go over the numbers. "Well Kate, is there anything that is on your mind that you would like to discuss?" I said. And before she could reply I discreetly put in a second question on purpose I had never asked before. "Is there anything I could be doing better to assist with any of your goals within the company?" I quickly asked. There was an uncomfortable silence after that question was asked. Clearly, no one had ever asked her that before and frankly I had never asked it myself. Don't get me wrong, I ask that question all the time in interviews and even just shooting the breeze with other associates on break. But this one was different because it was formal and it was just us two in the office. "I am not exactly sure what you mean by the second question?" Kate responded. "You seem to be a good boss so I don't have any complaints if that is what you are asking?" "Not exactly." I replied. I was not going to let her off the hook that easy. "I am going to be blunt with you Kate," I said (That has gotten me in trouble so many times). "You are one of the top associates amongst ALL the teams every month. No one ever has any issues with your work and your attendance and punctuality are near perfect. I never hear you say much and you don't seem to hang out with anyone in particular on breaks and lunches. You seem to be, as they say, all about your business and I respect that. But if there is anyone in this place that deserves to move up and further their career it is you. I have to ask Kate, am I the only one that has mentioned anything like this to you?" I said that last part even though I was pretty sure I knew the answer. At this point I knew there was going to be that long pause but I did not want to say anything else until she responded. After all, I may have said too much already. Then after that long pause Kate said something to me that caught me off guard because at the moment it seemed to be completely off subject. By the end of the conversation I soon realized why she asked. "You got kids sir?" she asked looking me dead in my eyes. I think that is the first time I ever saw her look anyone, including myself, directly in the eyes. I just never paid attention to it until that very moment. The interesting business woman showed me the windows to her soul, something that she clearly does not show many. "I have two." She said before I could answer. Since I had her speaking candidly I had to say something quickly as to not lose her again. "I don't have any children. What are your kid's names?" I asked. "Can't go wrong with that one." I was saying to myself. Well, there is Ben who is Two and Sam who is Five." Kate replied. It was at that point Kate began to truly speak to me. She spoke to me like she had not spoken a word in ages and just remembered she had the ability. The words were soft spoken but the material was powerful. I am not going to quote her because I do not remember everything word for word. I wish I could because you would hopefully feel those words as I did some years ago. She basically explained to me that if she received a promotion, that would include a pay increase. That pay increase would interfere with her public assistance check from the government. She explained to me how she had her first child at age 18. Sam was the light of her life. She said she never knew she could love anything as much as she loved him. But she was young and the father was not nearly as interested in raising a child as Kate was. He did what he could and came by to see Sam once a week but for the most part Kate did all of the heavy lifting. She made it a point to let me know her mother was a better grandmother than she ever was a mom to Kate. I think she emphasized that point to let me know that the child was loved and would never be neglected as she was growing up. She spoke of her two sisters, both much older than she. Her father passed away when she was just a child, she did not mention how and I did not ask. I just let her speak. I could tell she needed to and if I the one to listen then so be it. I did start it. Once she was done telling me her life story it was finally my turn to speak again. And the words that came out of my mouth could not have been more profound. With a partial smile I said to Kate, "I get it" and nodded my head in agreement. I did not agree, however, as you probably guessed but there was nothing else I could say. To me, her story was one of hopelessness. To her it was life. It was all she knew and no one ever asked why until that day I gave her a reason to tell me. Kate wasn't lazy. She wasn't a bad mom either. She could have just stayed at home and waited patiently at the mailbox for the next check. She told me she dressed up everyday like a professional because that is what she sees on TV when people have what she called "real" jobs. She was content with her life because that is all she ever knew. Her mother and her sisters all followed the same path, a job, but never a career. They had a life but never truly lived. Today that story rings even more true in my life as I will explain later. I would take Kate by the hand and educate her on what I have learned about life over the past few years. And what I have learned isn't difficult to teach. Instead I just said, "I get it."

Kate and I never had another conversation like that again. I did nothing and said nothing else about that talk. But it opened my eyes to the way some people thought. Some people just don't know any better. And if they don't have someone in their corner to show them a better way, chances are nothing will change. I made it a point to never stand by and watch anymore.

Not soon after that meeting between Kate and I things took a drastic turn at work….again. The satellite company did not renew their contract and a computer company was next on the list. That computer company fired me because I did not know enough about computers. They fired everyone that did not know enough about computers. A few months later they were gone and my former employer closed and did not reopen again. That large building is now a bingo hall. Oh the irony.

Chapter 2

CRASH ON J BIRD ROAD

Part I

"A ham sandwich Birdman!" I exclaimed, in response to my best friends constant eating out every day. "Make a ham sandwich sometimes for lunch and save a little cash man." I knew he was not going to ever do that. I don't know if he even knew how. Ok, that is a bit of a stretch but my best friend was the most spoiled individual I know. I will not speak his real name but if he ever reads this he will know it is about him. I don't have a problem with that. He would not either. Before I go any further, let me briefly explain why his name is not important. We never called him by his legal name. He was either called Birdman or J Bird on all occasions. "Crazy white boy" was used a few times but never by me. Normally by someone who just saw something they could not believe he just did. I left the use of his real name up to the adults in the room. By adults I mean his grandparent who raised him. J Bird had a tough beginning to this world when he was born. I guess that is why I took such a liking to him when we first met roughly 15 years ago. His mom was arrested and sent to prison for stealing a money order machine while he was still in her womb. When she gave birth to him, his grandparents took him in and raised him as if he was their own. They truly were the nicest people I had ever met. I lost touch his grandparents a few years ago and have regretted it ever since. You see, Birdman thought he was invincible and there was no one that was going to convince him otherwise, especially not his grandparents.

He was only 15 when we met so that would have made me in my early twenties. I was an assistant manager at a laser tag company. I did not know much about J Bird at that time. The other employees, that had been there longer than I, called him one of the "regulars". Everyone always found it so strange that every time he would be dropped off by his grandparents at the store, he would play laser tag for hours and hours each day. The thing that caught every ones attention was not the laser tag playing. It was two things. The first thing is he always had money to play as many games of laser tag as he wanted. And it was not cheap. The second thing and probably the weirdest was the fact that his grandparents would wait on him, outside the building in the car, the entire time he was playing. Keep in mind this was sometimes 4 and 5 hours at a time. Birdman played so much laser tag and was at the store so much, the manager decided to give him a job when he turned 16. You see, J Bird was home schooled by his grandparents. He was born with some kind of immune deficiency and was unable to be around large groups of kids. He was little in stature and had a really funny voice. I never asked but I had a feeling it had something to do with his mother's lifestyle while she was "with child". When J Bird started working with me that is when his life truly began. Overnight he went from spoiled little sheltered kid to one of the crew. And a crazy crew we were. We did not treat J Bird as a child although I think in hindsight we should have. He did not have to go to school and we did not either. He was now able to drive and he was receiving a paycheck. In other words, he was truly one of the guys. We use to go to the bowling alley every Saturday night after work. The crew consisted of regulars and employees. My brother and his wife would even come by every now and then and hang out. Birdman was in love with my brother's wife. He never said it but we all knew by the way he acted around her. Anyways, some of the crew would bowl but the Birdman and a couple of others including me would just go to have a few beers and talk about what ever. There was really no limit on how much we drank because the tab was not on us. And no it was not on J Bird either.

Allow me to explain. One thing all of us, regulars and employees, realized was that the equipment at the laser tag place was awful. I think when the owners bought the business they assumed this was going to be the hot spot in town forever. Unfortunately, once the newness wore off, the regulars and birthday parties were the main source of revenue for the company. And that was not enough to keep the equipment up to date. If memory serves me correctly, I think each one of those guns was 5000 dollars so rather than replace the old ones they would just get repaired. They were repaired over and over. Those things were repaired so much that a good number of them would not even last a whole game which was 15 minutes. If one of them did stop working we would have to pull the customer out of the game and give them a new laser. Why am I telling you all of this? Well, back when the company first opened, each sale was tracked by each individual laser that was used for a particular game. Once the lasers were no longer in good condition, it would sometimes take 2 maybe 3 lasers to complete a game. This mainly happened on Saturday nights when the lasers had been used so much the batteries were almost dead. It did not take us misfits long to realize there was now no way to track each customer's cash per game purchase. Long story short we developed a system and every Saturday night we would put it in place. Each game cost 5 dollars. Since there was no way to track the customers, whoever was working the register would put three paying customer's payments in the cash drawer and the fourth payment we would put under the register. So for every 4 customers we would generate 5 dollars of bowling and beer money. This only worked on Saturdays because the other days of the week the manager was there and the influx of customers just wasn't enough to take money without someone noticing. But Saturday, that was our "extra" paycheck only a few of us collected. And of course we justified the extra pay because of all of the flack we took from customers because our equipment sucked. We were so young and clueless back then, although in a very clever sort of way if I do say so myself.

You can imagine the complete and utter shock the Birdman must have felt hanging out with us. This crazy little soft spoken homeschooler was downing suds with people in their 20s on a Saturday night. And he was never carded because he was with us and we spent a lot of laser tag money. They did not care where we got the money from as long as it was green. We had this routine for, I would say, close to a year and then something changed. I knew change was inevitable as we could not be mischievous little crooks for the rest of our lives. This change, however, was unexpected to say the least.

My boss called me into the office on one of our many slow week days. Things had gotten so bad with the company we would sometimes work an entire shift during a weekday and not a single customer would come through the door, not good. Not saying that I had planned on working at that place for the rest of my life but all of us knew the end was coming at some point in time and it was going to be a big change for the crew. "Have a seat man." my boss said to me. "What's up boss?" I said shaking in my pants thinking the gig was up one way or another. Either we were going out of business or my little scheme had caught up to me. "How often do you see Bill on Saturdays?" My manager asked me. Bill was the area manager of the company. In the beginning, the laser tag business was booming. There were a total of 4 stores in our state. Bill was the area manager over 2 of them. His stores were about 100 miles apart from each other. "Bill usually comes in once or twice a month. It is usually an hour or so before closing time and he and his little girl usually go into the office for a few minutes." I responded. His little girl was about 3 or 4 years old and was a real sweetheart. We loved to see her way more so than Bill. She would come out of the office on her own while her daddy was working and we would walk her around that laser tag arena. "I think Bill is stealing from the company." My manager said. Now how in the world was I going to respond to that? "Really, what makes you say that?" I responded. Of course now I am thinking they have been tracking the sales a different way than I suspected and he is thinking Bill is the culprit. My boss began to explain, "Well man, this can't go any further than you, Jeremy and I ok? (Jeremy was the other assistant who had no idea of our little hustle) The corporate office in Tennessee reported to me that our quarterly finances were not adding up. At first I thought it may have been someone working for us stealing money until they continued and explained to me there was a discrepancy at both stores and a significant amount." You have no idea how deeply I exhaled once I realized it was not us he was talking about. Both stores would rule us out completely. This was something much bigger than a handful of twenties missing. "Whatever you need me to do I am here boss man," I said. "Well I have been thinking about that and this is what I came up with. I am going to the Spy Store and am going to set up a camera in the office facing the computer and the safe. I will probably need you and Jeremy's help," He replied. I thought to myself, that was a really good idea. It would not have caught us because we were doing our business at the register but to catch someone stealing in the office it would work perfectly. I am not going to draw this thing out any longer as this part of the story is suppose to be about the Birdman. Long story short, we set up the camera, filmed Bill for an entire month. He came in twice that month with his daughter both times. It turns out Bill was stealing. Not only cash but credit card info also. To top all of that off he was using his daughter as a distraction so none of us would come in the office while he was doing his business. I found out all of the details when my boss returned from headquarters. He said when they asked Bill about it he did not deny a thing. He did however say he was transferring the funds between the 2 stores so they would have similar profits. He said he did not want to lose one of them due to insufficient profits. I don't know if that was true or not but the reason I told you about all of that is because once that whole fiasco was over, I was done. I could no longer work there. I realized my conscience would not let me stay there after I just assisted in getting someone canned for doing the same thing I was doing, just on a much bigger scale. I left the company about a month or so after that and landed what some would call a corporate job at, you guessed it, a call center at a rental car company.

When I left the laser tag place, things changed. A couple of the guys got fired for getting caught doing the same thing I was doing. I guess they forgot what I had taught them. It was actually a good thing for J Bird because he became the assistant manager. At least I thought that was a good thing. Leaving that company was tough for me because it was so much fun but I knew it was time for me to get a real job. As for J Bird this would be the only real job he would ever have. And he was perfectly fine with that. His grandparents were fine with it also as it was only about 2 miles from their home. They never wanted him to be too far away. His grandparents did not mind him hanging out with the fellas as long as I was there. They trusted me with their grandson. But when I left the laser tag place, I was no longer able to keep a watch of him like they needed me to. Keep in mind about this time, although J Bird was still young, he was around 18 by now. He was an adult by age but was still such a child mentally from his years of entitlement provided by his grandparents. Having that job was everything to him but with the old crew gone, J Bird had to find new people to hang out with when I was not around. I had an 8 to 5 now so I could no longer hang out til 2 o'clock and sleep in because I did not have to work until 1:00 in the afternoon. He still had that luxury. And the main person he chose to hang out with all night turned out to be the beginning of the end. It was his mother. I am sure you guys remember that "stand up" lady right? All joking aside, she was actually a very sweet lady at least when I was around. She was one of those people that would do anything for you but did not really have much to give. J Bird absolutely loved going over to her place after work because she lived alone and he could drink and smoke pot with her anytime he felt the need. In the beginning I was glad he had a place to go. After all he was grown now and I would rather him there than hanging out with the wrong crowd somewhere else. His grandparents, however, knew better than that. They raised her and her son when she went to prison. They saw the path she took and were terrified he would stray from them and into her arms. That being said his grandparent would always try and get me to come over there so he would not go to his mom's house. They knew I could only do that on weekends but they were ok with that. They knew we would drink and smoke but for the most part it was harmless. Come to find out the reason they hated him going over to his moms was not so much her but the company she kept. And they were spot on with those concerns. Over the next couple of years J Bird changed drastically. Not his physical appearance, but his personality. He stopped staying at his grandparent's house for days at a time and would just stay with his mom. I started hanging out over there sometimes simply because he was not coming home and I still wanted to make sure my friend was ok. One day when I stopped by unannounced his mom was not there but he was there with someone I had not met before. This time we were not going to smoke a joint or down some beers though. J Bird had graduated to pills. And the pill man was there to oblige. I remember talking to J Bird one day soon after that and advised him to slow down. You have to remember he thought he was invincible. And the wakeup call that was on its way should have been enough proof that he was not.

As close as J Bird and I were and as much as I tried to look out for him, I don't think he ever really looked up to me. After all I had not accomplished much in my life. I was not the most popular person he knew and I sure was not the ladies man others would look up to. I think his grandparents were the main reason we stayed so close for so long but his idol was someone else. The person he always wanted to be was my former boss and his current boss of the laser tag place. J Bird loved the fact that everyone was terrified of the boss (Let's just call him that as I don't want him to come looking for me...just kidding). My former boss was awesome and had an intimidating attitude. He actually ended up buying the laser tag place once the owners decided they were tired of losing money. He not only bought that store but bought the store next to it to make it even larger. To describe the boss a little bit, he was this really buff Italian guy. He and his girlfriend were very athletic and I am pretty sure Birdman was in love with her also. Once he bought the store he asked J Bird if he would help him manage it. Since J Bird had nothing else to do he jumped at the chance. That was probably one of the happiest days of his life. When the boss was not there he was really in charge now. No corporate, just the two of them. J Bird also did the hiring now and he loved that. He loved the responsibility and treated that place as if it was finally his. I have to say I was happy for him. But one thing the boss did not know was when the store was closed at night, the Birdman was going down a really bad path. I would have to say without that place and myself I honestly don't know how things would have turned out for the Birdman. Now I can't speak for his early years and how his grandparents spoiled him but the years I remember, they went way too far for a grown man. When J Bird got that new gig, his grandparents bought him an, almost, brand new Maxima. The only reason it was not brand new is because he wanted the one that was exactly like the Boss mans and he got it. I was very against this decision because I knew he drank and drove, did drugs and drove and that car would fly. I mean it was so fast I had never seen anything like it. Not to mention he had just recently wrecked his first car driving like an idiot drinking. I happened to be with him on that night and none of us should have survived. But we did survive and now he has a newer, faster car. I guess his grandparents forgot about that little incident. Look out everybody!

That auto accident was not the crash this book's title is referring to. Although that would have been fitting, had things not gotten so much worse. About 2 months after J Bird took over the show, something so asinine happened I could not believe it when I heard. I did not find out until after this event, but J Bird actually hired that pill head I met at his moms house. I did not hang out with him nearly as much after he started his new gig because I did not want to be a distraction, good or bad, until I felt I would not be. Mrs. Shaw calls me one afternoon and tells me J Bird spent the night in jail. Although I was not shocked in the least, the reason he went to jail was just crazy. The store he was running sometimes had after hour's events for customers, mainly church groups and the like. The groups would stay up all night eating pizza and playing laser tag. Well this particular lock in J Bird and his pill head friend worked the overnighter. They get the bright idea to get all drunk and hopped up on pills so the night would go by faster. They were going to be there until 6 am after all with a bunch of screaming children. Well, sometime in the middle of the night the two of them decide to go out of the back of the building (in the middle of a laser tag match by the way) and climb up the service ladder to the roof. To paint the picture, the store is in a strip mall and at the very end of the mall is a movie theater with a glass atrium. They walked all the way to the theater, while on the roof, and started busting the windows out. All I can picture is the shards of glass falling 40 feet to the lobby floor and shattering into a million pieces. Well, even though it was 2 o'clock in the morning and no one was at the mall except them and the lock in customers, most places have these things called alarms for instances such as the one J Bird and company found themselves in. By the time they ran all the way on the roof back to the store the police were already there. One was in the front and one was in the back. The one in the back kindly escorted them down the ladder to the police car. J Bird had to give the keys to the cops just to close the store up. Wow is all I could think when I heard that story.

I am going to end this chapter for now but we will be returning at a later point in this book. I am getting a little too heated just thinking about it. You have not heard anything yet regarding J Bird's ultimate crash.

Chapter 3

ENTITLEMENT VS. EMPOWERMENT

Entitlement

1. the act of <u>entitling</u>.
2. the state of being <u>entitled</u>.
3. the right to guaranteed benefits under a government program, as Social Security or unemployment <u>compensation</u>.

J Bird and Kate have as many differences as they do similarities. One is black, one is white. One is male, one is female, one is from money and the other is not. They both don't mind working either. The most glaring similarity, however, is their entitled mentalities. And that mentality is an ultimate detriment to both of them and society as a whole. Neither of them is lazy, so let's not go there. I know there are many entitled people out there who are lazy but I do not have the time or the patience to deal with that right now. This book is not about that. Remember the saying I always, and still do say, "I can teach you anything you need to know about the job but I can't teach you to be here on time. That is out of my hands". No one can really make you do anything. And enablers make that even more difficult for those of us who want someone to succeed in whatever they dream possible. Whether it is Kate's check from the government or the Birdman's credit card from the grandparents, it is the same thing except for one small difference. One of them is rewarded for mediocrity from tax payers and the other is rewarded from granddad's wallet. You hear about stories like this from all walks of life. It is not a black thing or a white thing. It is something that starts with good intentions that, if it goes unmonitored, can become the downfall of a society. I could not help J Bird because of his grandparents. I could not compete with them. I hope Kate found that person that I wish I could have been for her, but I did not "get it" at the time we spoke. I can't do anything for either one of them anymore, but since then I have spoken to many others about my observations. Now don't get me wrong, I have been criticized and called every name in the book simply because I am stepping into a very sensitive subject some feel I don't belong. These people are mostly the uninformed and the enablers. But I made a promise to myself a few years back that I am going to speak my mind. If someone loses at this game called life it is NOT going to be because of me.

Being entitled and being poor are both states of the mind. Don't let people with power determine your state of mind. Use your mind's power against those who make a very good living telling you what is best for you. If you are not sure what is best for you do some research. Don't let a politician give you the answer. It is their job to convince you they know best, that's how they get paid. Do the leg work and convince you. You have to understand, everyone is different and the wants and needs of others may vary differently from your wants and needs. And they are especially different from people giving you advice for their own personal benefit. Do you know the difference between being poor and being poor and comfortable? The poor and comfortable person has a much longer road to recovery (Yes I said recovery). The poor and comfortable person has something to lose. The poor person does not. Have you ever heard the saying, "When you got nothing, you got nothing to lose?" I think deep down everyone wants to better themselves and create a better life for their families, but if it is not required, where is the motivation for some? The person without the help given to them will have to go find it. And find it they will. If they pay attention and work hard, people will respect you more knowing how hard you worked to get where you are and where you started from. Use that to your advantage. And if you do make it tell that story to others you know. Don't run for office and give back to your community by telling them it is not their fault. You succeeded. What makes you better than them? What makes you think they are not capable? You only make their lives worse in the long run feeling like victims. But by the time that happens you have moved on to bigger and better things. That community center you helped build? Your kids won't be playing in it by the time it is complete because you are now big time and have moved to the suburbs. You will show up for the ground breaking and the grand opening, but you will not stay. And why would you? You have made it.

Notice at the beginning of this chapter I put the definition of the word entitlement, but not the definition of empowerment. Empowerment is a word that does not need its meaning given to you. Find it for yourself and start there.

Let me be perfectly clear. I am in no way perfect, but things I learned on this tiresome journey will live long after I am gone. And I have many regrets. I regret that I spent almost all of my twenties trying to save a spoiled brat who needed my help but it was a losing battle. And I did not spend any of my twenties helping and educating the ones I could reach. I am no saint believe me. I have made more mistakes than you can possibly imagine. I could fill this book up with them but what would be the point? I learned from them no matter how painful they were. I do not live in a fantasy land. I understand there is always going to be poor people and some of them need to be taken care of. But how many of them honestly need to be taken care of forever? What makes this country great is we have the resources to take care of the needy. Some countries do not. But those resources did not come out of thin air. They came from empowered individuals. I am not asking you to build a country. Start with building you and then your family. The sky is the limit from there.

The reason I put the main focus of my two stories on J Bird and not Kate is for a very simple reason. I did nothing for one and everything for the other. And the decision I made was with the person that did not want to be saved. J Bird's story is truly an amazing one and it needs to be told. It was a major part of my life. But what

I learned most from the Birdman is my adult life did not truly begin until that chapter was closed. It did not make me a Republican but it definitely showed me what can happen with too much "assistance". Hard work well… works! Just ask the politicians that don't think you can do it. Everyone grows up physically but not everyone grows up mentally. You are going to become an adult whether you like it or not. Barring any mental illness, if you murder someone at age 18 you will be tried as an adult. You might as well start acting like one and you may avoid that scenario.

Chapter 4

WORK SMARTER, NOT HARDER

In the beginning of this book I mentioned I was a supervisor for a large technology call center. Well, my real working career did not start there. After I left the laser tag place, I ended up working for a call center at an international rental car company. That was actually my first "real" corporate job but I really did not consider my position corporate. The only thing corporate about it was I had to wear a tie everyday and could only have hair that did not touch my collar. I always found that strange considering we did not see any customers all day. I soon realized that was just the corporate way as I got older. Long story short, I did absolutely nothing most days and collected a pay check. This was a new department that the company created and asked one of my laser tag "regulars" to run it. He had been with this company for years and knew I would be able to handle it. After all, he saw some of the things as a manager I had to deal with at the laser tag store. The pay was nice for a youngster like me. I even brought my brother in as he was working at a shoe store at the time and was really impressed by my first pay check. Not to mention he had his first child on the way and was recently married to the young lady I mentioned when speaking about the bowling alley earlier. My brother was a salesman by heart. I think he got that trait from my father. I, however, did not. After about a year at the call center my brother took on a job in the car sales division. That was right up his alley and he actually worked his way up to Area Manager. He made that company his career and I was happy for him. I, on the other hand, was miserable. So miserable after a few years of doing nothing I tried my hand at the rental portion of the business. This is the part of the business where as they say, "the rubber hits the road". I was told by everyone I spoke too before leaving the call center that, "sales were everything in rental." I guess I was so ready for a change I did not take that to heart. I started out on my new venture an excited new rental associate.

It WAS all about sales and I was terrible at it. I use to continually tell myself, "How am I suppose to convince someone into buying rental insurance when the insurance they have already will cover the car?" I never grasped the concept of selling something I would not purchase myself. That is why I sucked as a salesman. Everyone loved me and thought I was such a good guy. I think they did not fire me because of that. Instead of firing me they gave me the opportunity to go back to the call center. As much as I hated to admit it that was not where I wanted to be but knew beyond a shadow of a doubt rental was going to get me fired.

After about a year in rental, here I was back at the call center. I did that for about another year and after that turned in my 2 week notice. I had no plans but had a little money saved up so I decided to call it quits and start completely from scratch. I thought to myself, "Maybe my mom was right about that whole college thing."

I said to myself when I left that place I was never cutting my hair again. And I have not in since then. I also said I would never shave again but that lasted about a week, until my face itched like I had never felt before. I remember at first, never cutting my hair again was kind of a statement to my previous job making me keep it cut like I was still in middle school. I still have that hair currently at age 38 and now am afraid to cut it because I don't think it will grow back. It honestly has not grown anymore in a few years. I think my scalp thinks my brain did not get the memo. But I like my long hair. It has been a part of me for so long I could not imagine myself without it. And it has not hindered my career in any way, shape or form. Although it could have a couple of years ago but I will get to that job in a few minutes. So like I was saying before, I left that job after a few years, because I was going nowhere and I knew there had to be something else out there for a guy with a C average high school diploma and no college experience. I knew the pickings would be slim but after about a week of lounging I started looking again. During my search I realized something very important. I had set myself up for either success or failure. I did not have the money or time to get any type of formal education and frankly I did not want to. I hated school and my previous job so rather than be miserable for the rest of my life I just jumped. I intentionally placed my back against the wall. I knew if I never left that job I would stay there forever. It is hard to get fired from a job where you don't really do anything. That did not mean upper management would not eventually find out and dissolve the department. And a couple of years later I heard through the grape vine that is exactly what happened. So looking back, I think I did the right thing. I just should not have done it so hastily without a plan. Anyways, after about a month, the money was drying up and I was starting to get desperate. Low and behold as I was driving to the hot dog place to spend some more money that I did not even have, I ran across this big building with a blue roof. I had driven by it countless times but never really thought anything of it, until I was desperate. The parking lot was full so I knew there was something going on that was worth my attention. I parked my car, walked in the building and that was the beginning of my technical career. I said hello for the first time to the job where Kate and I met.

When I walked in I was asked to have a seat and if I had about an hour to take a preliminary test on the computer. I was saying to myself at that time, "I just came in for an application. I have bacon cheese dogs in the car." Nevertheless I decided to stay. After about 15 minutes, I was called in to the computer room. The test was fairly simple I remembered. It was basic computer questions and some typing skills tests. I was in no way a complete novice to computers but a lot of that stuff I have to admit I did not know. This is where things get a little strange. Once I was done with the test, I was immediately escorted into a room with a supervisor sitting at the desk. The interview was right then. I was asked the basic interview questions such as what interested me in the job and am I used typing and talking on the phone. It lasted maybe 10 or 15 minutes and the young lady told me she would recommend me to be hired and human resources would be contacting me in the next few days with my start date. She said it would be a month of training in a class with other new associates and then we would start. The training was paid which was great because I was almost out of money and my bacon cheese dogs were now cold (They are just not the same reheated). The first place I went to was my mother's house. I had to tell her the good news. The first thing she said was,You went to an interview dressed like that?!" I had to explain to her I had no intentions of going to an interview. I just went in to get an application. And I had to agree with her I looked pretty sloppy. I actually looked like a guy who had not had a job in a month actually. So I guess I fit the part.

I started working at the technical call center about a week after that. This time I was dressed more nicely but I was never one for fashion in the first place. Even as I am typing this story years later, I could not tell you when the last time I bought a piece of clothing or a pair of shoes. Those items were always my gifts of choice on Christmas and my birthday. And they still are to this day.

I am going to run through this part pretty quickly as you already know the end to this job adventure. I really want to focus on the beginning. It was in the first couple of month that I learned something that would change the way I looked at work. Now the job was absolutely awful. I worked at a call center prior to this one but at my old job I was normally the one making the calls when I did have a call to take. This one, however, was nothing but incoming calls all day, from the time you clocked in until the time you clocked out. It was not easy whatsoever. Not to mention, I was not very good at it to start out. I started off way too nice and was on each call way too long. Not to mention I was not resolving many issue to boot. During my first month on the phones, I missed 3 days of work. Not because I was sick or anything, but because the job sucked. I was not off to a good start at all. I was on break one day soon after I returned from "being sick" and that is when I started paying attention to what was actually going on around me. I was sitting in the lunchroom by myself, as usual, and just started listening and watching my surroundings. I did not have to ask anyone if they liked their job. I already knew the answer to that. So what I decided to do was go over to one of the supervisors and ask a few questions. I did not go to mine because she was probably still pissed I missed 3 days in a row. I remember walking up to a supervisor named named Candy. Candy was a very good looking woman who had been with the company for 5 years. Since I had been there, I noticed, she really did not hang around the associates, just the other supervisors. Another thing I noticed in the short time I was there was she only hung around the veterans who had been there a while. I knew she was going to be surprised by me approaching her desk but I said to myself, "Here goes nothing."

"It's Candy right?" I asked the young lady sitting at the desk. "Actually it is Cindy," She replied. "Great job idiot," I said to myself. As I mentioned earlier, when I spoke of me being a supervisor, the managers had offices and the supervisors sat on the main floor with their teams. That being said, I had to be somewhat discreet as to not let anyone else hear. "Can I help you?" Cindy replied. I responded, "Absolutely and thanks in advance for any information you can give me. I am more so looking for some advice and not just a simple question. I started here a couple of months ago and could not help but notice, out of the 22 folks that started with me in my training class, only ten of them are still here. I know the job is difficult but it beats working outside in the heat or no job at all. Not to mention it pays above minimum wage. Can you give me a little insight?" Cindy paused for a second and then said, "It is interesting you mentioned that. I have been here for years and have often wondered the same thing. When I started things were a little bit different as the job was new to the area and everyone was excited to have a place to go to work right here in this area. Once the newness wore off after a couple of years, however, it began to develop a reputation around the community. That reputation became one of this place just being a temporary job until something better came along. People would joke, and still do, about how everybody they know has worked here at one time or another. I am saying that to let you know the perception about this place on the outside has made its way inside those doors. Long story short 80 percent of the people you see out here on the floor do not take this job seriously. They get here when they want to and never come back from breaks on time. They are rude to the customers and I swear we fire more people than we hire. I think the biggest attrition factor we have is folks just stop coming to work altogether." As I listened to Cindy I could hear the frustration in her voice and it set off a light bulb upstairs.

When I worked at the call center for the rental company, hardly anyone ever left. The people there were content to stay, not only because the job was easy, but it was with a great company. The benefits were great and they even had profit sharing. This company however was different. No one working here had benefits, starting out, or a sense of a possible career opportunity. The company was not known in this area before it came and as far as most in my city were concerned it was only known as, "the place everyone has worked for at some point in their lives." Little did they know, it was actually a very large worldwide corporation. Perception is truly everything. Now I could not speak for anyone else at this place but from what I noticed so far, I could move up in this place without a lot of technical skill. I concluded after our conversation, a good work ethic and customer service skills is all it really took to move up. Knowing this information I set my plan into place.

For the next 6 months I never missed a day of work, always showed up 30 minutes early and volunteered for any extra duties that my supervisors needed assistance with. That part was easy and somewhat fun. I saw so many people come and go within that 6 months and everyone that left was another one I no longer had to compete against. And the new ones hired in I now had seniority over. Not to mention I was making a name for myself with the managers. Not the supervisors but the managers. I was about 7 months into my job when my then boss came to me and told me of two supervisor positions that were about to come open. Now I will say this, of all the people that came and went in this building, supervisors rarely left. I appreciated my boss' heads up, but she filled me in on something that I was not aware of. She explained to me I met all of the qualifications to apply but one. And that was my call statistics. My customer service statistics were great but I had never once met all of my monthly goals as far as talk times, hold times and such. Mainly talk time was my biggest problem. So I had a month to get that one in order before I could apply for a supervisor position. Since the position had not even posted yet I knew I had time. And that is exactly what I did. I put a new strategy in place to help me as the way I was taking was not working. After analyzing my problems I noticed my friendliness was just too "friendly." Customers loved to get someone like me on the phone considering the last person they spoke with was probably very rude and straight to the point. They would get me on the phone and make sure any other questions they could think of were answered because they knew they would not get attitude from me. Well, that is precisely why my customer service scores were so good but my talk time was not. I had to find a way to find that balance without upsetting customers. And I did it in truly hustler fashion as I had done most things in my life up to that point.

I realized if I could find a way to take only easy calls then this would be a breeze, but how in the world could I determine what calls I would get? Well I could not. But what I had been doing was coaching some of the newer associates that had just recently gotten on the phones. Coaching required not taking calls at all but instead sitting with them and listening. I was chosen to do this because of my customer service skills, not my stats. Normally I would sit with various new associates for half the day and take calls the latter half. So this is what I did. Not taking a full days worth of calls due to coaching was not necessarily an advantage. But it could be if the small amount of calls I took were all short ones. So when I was in the process of coaching I would log in as myself when a call came in that I knew was going to be short and log in as the new user when I knew it was going to be long. The supervisor never noticed and the user did not care because a new associate's talk time is going to be high regardless. The other thing I did to give me added insurance was anytime I saw there was a big outage somewhere, I would make sure to be on the phones no matter what time of day it happened. Those calls only last 30 seconds at best because we knew there was a bigger issue and there was nothing that could be done from our end. In the end it all paid off. I met my stats for the month, 2 positions were posted and I got one of them. Whew!

Well everyone knows pretty much what happened after that if you read the beginning of the book. That was not the end of my working career but it was one of the most memorable. And it was at that point I realized if you pay attention to the little things and ask the right questions to the right people, you will not waste your time finding out what really matters on your own. I heard a quote a while back from someone and I can't even remember who it was (Go figure) but it said, "Never take advice from anyone that does not have what you want." Someone that use to work at that job with me also had a profound saying, "Man, working at this job is like a big party without the drinks." Both of those statements rang true on so many levels I laugh just thinking about it.

Chapter 5

ADDIE'S DAZZLING MOTHER

All I remember hearing is one loud but very short scream. I think she remembered her kids were in the next room and quickly muffled it as not to startle us. I was probably around 12 at the time. My brother and I were a year and 9 months apart. He was the oldest of the three and my sister was close to turning 2. I remember my mother coming into me and my brother's room and sitting my sister in between us. She did not say a word. She just quickly went back out and shut the door. I don't remember if my brother or my sister was awake at this time, but I know I was. A few minutes after she left the room I remember hearing beeps. Not the beeps you hear when a truck backs up. It was more like the beeps of machines you would hear in a hospital. At that time I really had no idea what it was. I just knew something was going on and I was not going to move until mom said so. I don't know how much time had passed but my mom eventually did come back in the room and made sure all three of us were up. Then she said something that made me realize something was definitely wrong. "Let's all say the Lord's Prayer," She said. "Can you two say it with me?" We all huddled together in the center of the bed, my sister in the middle, and then my mom began to pray. My brother and I, although confused, then started saying that prayer we had heard probably over a hundred times with her.

"Our Father, which art in heaven, Hallowed be thy Name. Thy Kingdom come. Thy will be done in earth, As it is in heaven. Give us this day our daily bread. And forgive us our debts, As we forgive our debtors. And lead us not into temptation, But deliver us from evil. For thine is the kingdom, The power, and the glory, Forever and ever. Amen."

I can't imagine going to sleep after that but I think I did. If I did not I don't remember anything else until that next morning. My sister was still sleeping in between my brother and I when my mom walked into the room and gave us the news. "Daddy didn't make it." She said. Then she hugged us, left the room and shut the door. I have no idea how long me and my siblings sat there after she left, but one thing I do remember was eventually walking into the living room. I remember my neighbor from down the street being there. She was standing next to my mom. My mom was sitting on the couch with her feet curled up under her. Her hand was under her chin as her elbow lay upon the arm rest. She looked tired. She looked defeated. She had a long night. I remember later that morning looking out of the living room window and seeing two guys in suits and ties picking up the dealership car that my father use to drive home each night. I think that is when it hit home to me that this was as real as it gets. When they drove away I knew they were not coming back, and neither was my father....ever. I assumed that was the look of defeat I saw on my mother's face as she was sitting on that couch. She was much older and I am sure it sunk in way quicker to her. And it was way more real.

We are going to now skip all of the food and people and hugs and handshakes that went on for the next couple of days. All of that happens during every death, but this one was different, because my father was so young. He was younger than I am now. My mom told me later it was a heart attack and it came completely out of nowhere. It is different when you have time to prepare. This caught everyone by surprise.

The funeral was huge. There were so many people I was overwhelmed. I even saw my principal. That was kind of weird. I did not see my mom much during the days leading up to the funeral. I know she was probably busy with all of the arrangement and whatever else a person does after losing a loved one. My siblings and I stayed at my neighbor's house for a couple of days after the whole thing happened. We would have just been in the way. The viewing of the body before the funeral was powerful to say the least. After everyone viewed my father in his casket and sat down, it was time for the family. My mom was not there next to us and I remembered wondering where she was. After my brother and I sat down, I looked around for my mother. She was coming down the aisle dressed in all black carrying my sister. Everyone else had already sat down. She walked up to the casket and kissed my father. And then it happened. As she walked away my sister turned to the casket and started calling for "daddy". This just ripped every ones heart clean out of their chests. I even remember hearing one lady behind me whisper, "She should not have done that."

It was a powerful scene. And to this day I don't know why my mother did it the way that she did. Was it to cause a scene? I doubt it. Was it to prove a point to show how much my father was loved? Who knows? Whatever the reason was, after that day, my mom was never the same. I knew then that woman I saw sitting on that couch the morning after my father's death was no more. That woman sitting on that couch died with my father. It was time to move on and move on she did in the most wonderful way anyone could imagine.

I said when I started writing this that I was not going to speak of anyone in my family. But after this past Sunday I really had no choice. I had to tell you about my father's death to help you understand how a traumatic event can change someone. It can change them for the better or for the worse. And my mother knew she was on her own now and had a job to do. And that job was raising us. My mother has always been perfect to me even before that life changing experience. I have never heard her curse. I have only seen her drink one time and it was a glass of wine at my wedding reception. And she never has a bad word to say about anyone unless it is in good humor. Now my mom will tell you to this day that she is not perfect, but I beg to differ. She is perfect in my eyes because she cherishes life more so than anyone I have ever seen. She cherishes everything about it and I am going to give you a quick example of that before I can continue on with my story. It will give you a little insight into who my mom actually is. And why they lived so long. Since it is close to Mothers Day I figure what the heck.

Just this past Saturday I was assisting my wife and daughter with a youth day yard sale at church. I would say I had been there maybe an hour when I received a text from my mother. It was a group text and it was sent to the whole family that lives here in this city. The text read, "Addie passed this morning. Graveside services on Sunday, May 4 at 2 pm in the flower bed as she joins Dazzle. Reception to follow to celebrate 28 years of life." Dazzle and Addie were my mom's cockatiels. They were actually my family's birds. A cockatiel's lifespan in captivity is generally given as 16–25 years, though it is sometimes given as short as 10–15 years. Don't tell that last part to my mom, or to Dazzle and Addie for that matter. I told my wife about it after getting the text and she gave the expected, "Awe that is so sad. Tell her I am sorry." That was the correct response and the one that was expected, but she did not know the significance of this as I did. Dazzle had passed a couple of years before and the family assumed Addie was going to go soon after as they had been together for so many years. You hear that a lot with married couples who had been together for decades. But Addie decided to hang around for 2 more years. I guess she just wasn't ready quite yet. We took these birds in when they were already 5 years old. A lady that mom was in a smocking class with could no longer keep them and my mom decided to take them off of her hands. I can remember I was the one that drove to pick them up. You see, I was 16 and had just gotten my driver's license. That was going to be the longest drive I had made and I was excited about it. Who knew way back then that I would be writing about these birds and the end of an era.

We had many pets over the years, dogs and cats, turtles and fish. Never anything that looked like a mouse though. My mom was terrified of those. I can remember years ago my mom accidentally touched one in the laundry room and my dad actually had to come home from work to calm her down. Yes crazy I know, but you can see why we never pushed the envelope about a hamster or anything. The birds however outlasted all of them by a long shot. The next closest one was Stewart the cat. Stewart was actually a girl (Go figure) and we had her for years. We did not realize she was a girl until she had kittens. And ironically that is the name of my step father. I just realized that wow. Strictly a coincidence I assure you. I don't really have much to say about the birds because, well, they were birds. They loved it when Andy Griffith would come on because they chirped along to the whistle every evening, for as long as I can remember. One was gray and the other was yellow. Dazzle, the grey one, loved to escape the cage and fly around. Addie never really found that exciting so never really did. And if Addie did escape, it was just to sit on the top of the cage on the wooden handle until one of us put her back in.

When I pulled up after church last weekend my step dad was sitting on the porch and the sprinkler was watering the front yard. I was the first to show up for the ceremony so I assisted him in digging the whole in the flowerbed next to Dazzle's grave. "Do you think it is big enough?" He asked. I replied, "I am not sure what is she buried in?" "Go take a look in the living room. She is in a box on the coffee table." He said. So I walked into the house and there she was. The box was resting on the coffee table, on top of a pedestal kind of like a trophy would be. A picture of both birds sat on the table in front of the pedestal. I am not sure if the whole trophy like presentation was planned but it would not have surprised me because I know my mother. I also noticed the nice spread on the dining room table. Addie got the good dishes. And she deserved them I think. Understand we did not make a big deal out of it when Dazzle died. There was no grave side service. Looking back I think we should have but nothing really changed when we lost her. Addie was still alive, the cage was still there and the chirping still continued. But now it had stopped forever. Forever is different and my mom was well aware of that. I was well aware of that. So I get the box and take it outside knowing it is not going to fit into that whole. But I wanted to satisfy my stepdad's opinion. "Nope doesn't fit," He replied. And I responded, "Agreed." I put the box back on the table and was grateful my mom did not pull up as we were testing the size of the hole. I mean, you don't test out a casket before putting it into the ground right? And if the box was on that pedestal for a reason I did not want her to see me moving it. So by the time the hole was dug appropriately the other family members started showing up and the ceremony started soon afterwards.

There were meatballs, ham sandwiches, ham sandwiches on pita bread, spinach dip and a lot of other finger foods at the pre ceremony. I noticed there was no chicken and had to make sure I pointed out that that would be offensive to the deceased had we had some. I always have to keep things a little on the humorous side. I think I may have gone a little too far though when my mother asked where my sister's husband was. She said he did not come because he was not feeling well. I then promptly replied, "What does he have, Bird Flu?" You have to understand my family. We find humor in everything and I even got a laugh from my mom. As significant as this service was my mom knew to expect the jokes. But she also knew we would not miss it for the world. We knew how much it meant to her. After eating we all sat in the living room circled around the coffee table where Addie lay. My mom then told the whole story about the birds. Much of it is what I mentioned earlier in this chapter, so I will not repeat that part. She did mention something that had happened just a couple of days before Addie passed that I found interesting. "I knew she was getting ready to go." She said. She continued, "The day before yesterday Addie got out of her cage and flew around the den on 4 separate occasions." Remember Addie was the one that never left the cage, and certainly never flew. As the birds got older, along with the 28 year old cage, the food and water dish compartment would not hold the dishes anymore because the tabs were broken. So to feed the birds we would just open the cage and do it that way. That in turn left 2 holes at the bottom of the cage that Dazzle would sometimes crawl through to get out. Addie never did though. But she did it 4 times in one day. My mom then explained to all of us why she thought Addie escaped. "You know," She started. "I think that was the last thing on Addie's bucket list. She wanted to get out of that cage and fly as long as she could. And when I put her back, she just got out and did it again and again." Everyone chuckled at that notion but we all knew she meant every word she said. After the stories, we all went outside and buried Addie next to her long time companion. And of course my mom had to take it way over the top when she played, "On The Wings of Love" by James Ingram as my step dad, shaking his head, put the dirt back in the hole.

That was my mom. She is my hero, if for nothing else, simply for moments like these. Our wives and husbands never really got it and that was fine by us. If they did get it, it would not have been as special. I know this story has nothing to do with this book. But it just happened and I had to put it out there. Cut me some slack.

Happy Mother's Day Mom

Chapter 6

FIND YOUR WAY, FIND YOUR "WHY"

I realized after writing the last chapter that trying to take on an endeavor like this is going to be near impossible without including my family. It is the story of my life, and my family is a big part of that. I had to take a few days off from writing after the chapter about my mom. It overwhelmed me to write something like that. It was a very powerful moment in my life and I did not realize how powerful until I wrote it down on these pages. If you have not noticed yet I am very close to my family. My family is everything to me and although we like to have fun, as most families do, we are also all about taking care of business and each other. I am sure you have heard the saying, "work hard, play hard." That is us. We believe in rewarding our successes and overcoming our failures. And we all strive to continually lift each other up. Life is tough but having a support system as I do makes things less stressful on most occasions. But if you screw up, that same support system can make you feel terrible because you know you let them down. I honestly think that is probably the biggest reason for my successes. I always want my mom to be proud of me along with everyone in my family. That includes the family I married into. The funniest part about my entire family is they are ALL Democrats. I am the lone Republican. I learned a long time ago that when you are outnumbered like that, with family, you don't make the mistake of taking on all of them by yourself. That is a battle no one can win. Now a day, when I talk politics, I try to keep it on a one on one basis. And if there is some partying going on I try not to mention it at all. One of the things that intrigue me the most about my family is the fact that I have absolutely no idea why they are Democrats. They believe in practically everything I believe in. They are all hard workers. They hate other people's hands in their pockets. They believe if they can do it, anyone can. We have all overcome so much I don't understand why they are with the party of, "let us do it for you." I just don't get it. And what is funny is when I talk to them on a one on one basis they get it. I make sense to them. Now don't get me wrong, I am a Republican but I am not a Conservative. I believe in less government but I am not a traditionalist. If you ever meet me you will know that just from my appearance. I am of the simple belief that the more money an individual can hold onto, (Less taxes) the more that individual will spend thus boosting the economy. It seems pretty simple to me. The more money a business can hold onto, the greater the chance of growth and therefore the greater the chance of new jobs. That is not too complicated is it? I don't believe the minimum wage should be raised to ten plus dollars an hour. If this happens do you think Wal Mart will hire more people or let people go. They are in the business of making money as any "for profit" business. When my daughter turns 16 do you think she is going to be able to get a job if the minimum wage goes up to ten dollars an hour? Minimum wage is just that, minimum wage. Jobs that pay minimum wages are not meant to support a family. They never were meant for that and I don't know why that opinion has changed over time. Minimum wage is as low as you can legally get so the only way to go from there is up. Use that as motivation. Everyone had to start somewhere.

When I was fired from my previous tech job working at that call center, I already had an idea of what I wanted to do. A lot of people that left that company went to the same Fortune 500 company that I wanted to go to so I knew I had a few connections that could help me get my foot in the door. I knew all I needed was an interview. And that is exactly what I got.

I am not going to bore you with another story about my career. There really isn't much entertaining about it. Let's just say when I started at this new company I could tell after the first week that this is somewhere I wanted to be and stay. This place wasn't going anywhere. The only thing I was concerned about was would my same practices work in a place like this. I started at the bottom of the technology department, which was the Support Center, but the pay was more than I made as a supervisor at my old job. I knew these people meant business. And I also knew the competition was going to be tougher. Money tends to have that effect on a workplace. The job was a lot more challenging and the training was completely different. There was no training class this time. No time for that. And you had better know your basic computer skills because that was not taught either. Fortunately, even with no formal education, I had just enough computer knowledge from my old job to handle this one….barely. I was overwhelmed at first as I am with every job, but guess what? Those same practices worked. I paid attention to what my bosses wanted and found out what was really important to them. I made their jobs easier and volunteered for every possible after hours task available. Even if it was last minute I would still do it. This let them know they could count on me. After about 13 months (You had to stay in your department for a year before posting for other positions) I had made a name for myself and one of the other Vice Presidents came looking for me. I had built a good reputation. I did not have to interview for my next position. I was simply called into her office. She showed me what they did and asked if I was interested. Of course I said yes. I loved that job so much that I stayed for 3 years. Then something strange happened. My boss left that department and was transferred to my old department. This was the department that I initially started in. When she transferred she wanted to bring in a manager that she knew she could count on. Take a wild guess at who that was? You guessed it. I managed a group of about 23-25 technicians for the next two years. I saw my pay increase along with it. I was making more money than I ever thought I would make. It was not a lot, just a lot for me. After those 2 years were up, I ran into another manager in the break room one day and she whispered to me to take a look at the job posting site. I don't think I had ever really spoken to her before but I knew who she was. I went to the site and looked at the position and the only thing I saw was the salary. It was way more than I was making as a manager. Needless to say I went to my boss and told her that I was going to apply for it. After I applied for the new position, the hiring manager called me to her desk and when I got there she asked me 2 questions. She asked me if I liked technology and if the pay was enough? I said a resounding yes to both of those questions and she offered me the job right then and there. To top all of that, they upped the pay another few thousand dollars because they did not want me to come in making the minimum. Too crazy huh? Once again it is truly amazing how simple things can be if you just take a step back and see what is really going on, what is really important.

I told you I was not going to go on and on about my current job. I did not tell any specific stories or anything. I ran through this past 6 years in just a handful of words. I did it to prove a point. Since my initial interview with this company I have never technically interviewed for any job. People came looking for me because of my reputation. Reputation can get you a long way but you have to earn it. And once you earn it you have to protect it. Once again, I did not do anything special. But I proved to myself that my thinking works in any arena. And the most important thing is, ANYONE CAN DO IT! You just have to change the way you think and start hanging around people that want you to succeed. And more than anything, please don't let anyone tell you it is not your fault. Don't let them tell you, you were dealt a bad hand. You have to understand your failure is their success. Don't let them have that kind of power over you. What you need to do is find out the "why" in your life. Initially, my "why" was just to show myself it could be done without all of the credentials. Would the credentials have helped? Well, it probably would have made getting in the door a little easier, but not having those credentials helped me think outside the box. I also wonder if I would have worked as hard with that degree or expected success to come knocking on my door? Who knows because I sure don't.

Once I met my now wife a few years back my "why" was no longer just about me. One other thing this wonderful company I work for has given me was my wife. I would have never met her had it not been for this place as she worked here long before me. Her department downsized a couple of years ago and she was let go. Her and I both, to this day, still think it had to do with me and how my career was taking off. Whether it was or wasn't does not bother me because she has been a stay at home mom for the last 2 years. She loves it and as long as she is happy, I am happy. I do not have any children of my own. I never really wanted kids, for a few reasons, but my wife has 3 from a previous marriage. I adore them all. Two of them are grown now but we see them all the time. My stepson looks at me and loves the fact that his mom does not have to work. He is proud to have me as his stepfather and tries to mirror what I have done in my life. I have to say, he does a pretty good job of it. His girlfriend and his son both live with him and they are a great little family. He wants his girlfriend to go to school since he pays all of the bills anyway. Not to brag but I like to think it is because of me and his mother that he does the right things when it come to family. I like to think I am rubbing off on him. If he ever reads this, I want him to know whatever happens in his life, I am proud of whom he has become. My twelve year old ultimately has my heart though. I love the fact that my wife can devote all of her attention to her instead of a job. I would not say my daughter feels the same way but hey, she is twelve after all. I also have a third daughter who is twenty eight. Needless to say she has her own life now and a son of her own. I wish I had met her years before. Maybe then I would have kept her on the straight and narrow. Don't get me wrong, she is a good person. She just has made some decisions in her life that is making it harder for her to become who I know she really can. I take pride in the fact that she is working on it every day though. To end this chapter, those are my "why". Find yours and stop at nothing to give them the very best. They deserve it. And once again don't let anyone else tell you your goal is not reachable. This is the greatest country in the world. You should take advantage of it while you still can.

Chapter 7

CRASH ON
J BIRD ROAD

Part II

"He is going to kill either himself or someone else Mr. Shaw," I said. For the first time I spoke my mind around Mr. and Mrs. Shaw. His grand dad and I were sitting on the front porch at their house. I was drinking a beer, his grandmother was in the kitchen cooking and Mr. Shaw was sitting next to me in complete silence. I knew he was listening but he spoke not a word. They had just bailed J Bird out of jail and he was asleep in his room. I am sure he had a long night. I continued, "You and Mrs. Shaw have got to stop spoiling him." Still nothing was said. I never wanted to disrespect either of them because they were like a second family to me. I sometimes would visit even when J Bird was not there. It was so peaceful where they lived. They owned a parcel of land you would think would be in a rural area but the world grew up around them. That little paradise had not changed in decades but as soon as you reached the end of the road, the hustle and bustle of life awaited. But down that street, that was a different world. And the perfect place to raise a child it was. J Bird always took for granted what he actually had. The Shaws did not help. They were grandparents never meant to raise a child at their ages. Grandparents are supposed to spoil their grand children, but parents, no. Parents are supposed to be the teachers and guardians. J Bird never had that. I think deep down he cried out for it all the time but there was no one to listen. It was truly a sad state of affairs, today especially. I knew when he found out he lost his job he was going to go crazy. He was going to go crazier than he already was. It was not just about losing the job. He was going to lose it because he let down the one person he respected above all others, his boss. That conversation was not going to be pretty and at that time I still did not think J Bird knew what was about to happen. I don't think he had a clue that his job was gone and his life without it was just beginning. Just like that paradise he called home, change was a rarity for that household, but it was inevitable now. I honestly did not know what to expect when J Bird awoke. Dependency is a scary thing if that is all you know. Just ask Kate and the Birdman.

I decided to go home that evening before J Bird woke up. I had work the next day and had to get an early start in the morning. Let me set the time line for you, to avoid any confusion. I know I have jumped around a good bit so, as to not confuse you more, most of this saga with J Bird happened pretty much while I was working at the rental car place. I think the ending came along shortly after I started working at the technical call center. By the time I got to the place I am working at now I think all of it was over. I may be off by a few months but that is close enough. If you recall, when I was working at that rental car company, I wasn't exactly the most fulfilled person. I was not happy at my job, nor was I happy with my life. I felt like I was just barely making it. J Bird and my other friends gave me a sense belonging during that time in my life that my job could not give me. I say that just to give a little insight into what was going on in my head during this time. I had no idea where my life was going but I knew where J Bird was headed.

To my surprise, I did not hear from J Bird the next day. I decided not to call because I figured he was probably getting the news that he no longer had a job. Even if the boss man did not want to fire him there was no way he would be allowed back in the shopping center so it did not matter. Can you believe the only thing J bird ever knew, was coming to an abrupt end? Well I knew it was going to be hard for him but I remained optimistic that he would get over it eventually. He had overcome worse whether he believed it or not. I even thought to myself this might take him out of his "fantasy land." This might actually be the eye opener he has needed for years.

I did not hear from J Bird until the following day. He stopped by my house that afternoon when I was just getting off work. I use to always tell him not to come by the house right when I get off work because I needed time to wind down from a day of doing nothing at work. Today, however, I did not mind seeing him right after work. "What's up Birdman?" I asked. Birdman began to cry, "I lost my job man! What the hell am I going to do now?" "I don't know Birdman? Just take it one day at a time. It is not like you had to have that job. You will find something else dude trust me," I replied. "What about getting a job where you work?" He asked me. "Naw man you would not want a job like that. It would drive you crazy sitting at a desk for 40 hours a week," I said. In all honesty he would have driven me crazy if he and I worked at the same job. Especially I job like that where "free time" is basically all we had. I would not tell him that though. "I tell you what J Bird, try not to think about that right now and we will hang out this weekend. Just me and you and we will have a good time. How does that sound?" I asked. I thought it would be good for him just to kick back with me and only me. We had not really hung out like that for a little while, just the two of us. I just hoped he would make it to Friday without doing anything crazy.

Now this is the point in the story where I have to question my own sanity....again. I had two days to think of something cool to do for J Bird. I did not just want to sit around his house or my house or his mom's house. He had just been dealt a tough blow so I wanted to cheer him up. And after some thought, I figured out what I thought was the perfect plan. If you remember earlier in the story I mentioned J Bird having a crush on my brother's wife? Well by this time my brother and his wife had been divorced. She ran into a string of issues with drugs and it had gotten so bad that my brother could not take it anymore. He left her and took the kids with him. Not long after that, my former sister in law checked herself into rehab. From all that I had known and heard she was doing much better. I heard she was seeing someone else now and things were really looking up for her. She was even able to see her kids on a regular basis. Well I thought the person that J Bird would love to see the most was her. I also thought it would be good for him to see someone that had hit rock bottom only regain control of their life. So I made it up in my mind we were going to see her on Friday night. Of course I had to call and make sure it would be ok. She had known J Bird for as long as I had so I did not think it would be a problem. And it was not a problem. She actually was excited to see him and myself since it had been a while. That was great news. I did not tell J Bird of the plan until Friday night after he picked me up. "So what's the plan dude?" J Bird asked. I said, "Well Birdman, we are going to see someone you have not seen in a long time. Someone I know will cheer you up." "Who is it?" He asked. I figured now was a better time than any to tell him. "We are going over to Julie's house," I told him. Not only did J Bird know Julie from the after work outings we used to go on after work, he saw her all the time when we would go to my brothers house and when they would come over to my house to hang out. Julie was actually a part of the crew for a while until she started going off the deep end. "Wow I haven't seen her in years." This is going to be awesome! Does she know I am coming with you?" J Bird asked. "Yep, she knows and can't wait to see both of us," I replied. We stopped at the store on the way to pick up a 6 pack of beer. I knew Julie would not mind as she never really drank anyways. "Does she have a boyfriend?" J Bird asked, with so much excitement it was not funny. I chuckled and said, "Well I think she may be seeing someone but the last I heard of that was a month or so ago. So I really am not sure. We will see when we get over there." It was at that moment I knew I had made the right choice. I actually had not seen him so excited and anxious in a really long time. He was not thinking about that job at all right now and that was the plan all along.

When we pulled up at Julie's she was standing out on the porch smoking a cigarette. Julie was a pretty young lady. J Bird thought she was beautiful but I used to lean more towards her being "cute" rather than gorgeous. She was short, about J Birds height (and mine for that matter) and she had a very pretty complexion. Her mother was white and her father was black. You could tell the drug usage had taken a toll on her physically but, nevertheless, she was still a pretty lady. Her and my brother were married a few years and had 3 children together. At one point in time we were all just a big happy family of misfits, J Bird included. But everything changes with time. And drugs and alcohol speeds that time up drastically let me tell you.

"Birdman, you have not changed a bit! Get over here and give me a hug," Julie shouted from the porch. And J Bird was all too happy to oblige. I don't think Julie ever called him J Bird. She only called him Birdman. I just realized that. After J Bird's hug, I gave my former sister in law a hug and we proceeded to go inside the house. The home was just as I remembered. This was the same house they lived in for a while when they were married. She was the only one there at this time as this was not the weekend she had the children. I put the beers in the fridge while J Bird and Julie just talked away. They spoke like they had not seen each other in decades. And yes, he did tell her about losing his job. It did not, however, dampen his spirits. At that point in time I said to myself this was the best idea yet. He was not even thinking about the job. The three of us sat and chatted for hours just smoking cigs on the porch and J Bird and I drinking beer. It was quite fun to catch up. After a little while I realized this little idea I concocted for J Bird actually made me feel good also. What an evening. I think we ended up leaving Julie's house around 3 o'clock that morning. I ended up staying the night at J Birds and went home the next morning without waking anyone up. And as I left J Bird's little paradise, I patted myself on the back for a job well done. As you can probably guess my plan once again backfired.

Chapter 9 is where you will find out the conclusion of the Birdman's story. It is not a pretty one, nor a happy one. I will, however, say it was an inevitable one.

Chapter 8

HEARTS AND MINDS

Barrack Obama's back was against the wall when he first achieved the Office of the President of the United States. And I sincerely do not think it was because he was black. I actually think the color of his skin played a major role in how he became President. He garnered most of the young and minority voters in his first successful run at Commander in Chief. I personally think that showed how far along this country has come, as a people. Others, however, would like for you to think differently. Others would like for you to think if you disagree with any of the President's policies and you are Republican, then you are a racist. I have been called that before and I just shake my head. Not because I am offended, (Because I can't be. I would never give anyone that power) but because they just don't get it. Let me try to briefly explain why I am skeptical of most of President Obama's policies and when I am done please make up your own mind if I am a racist or a bigot.

Imagine this scenario for a moment. I have already told you I work for a very large company and I have been here for roughly six years. Lets also say I that previously I was the President of the History department at a renown university (Just pick one). After my first two years of working at this company the CEO resigns and it is time for the Board of Directors to choose a new one. Let's now say I was chosen because I made all of these promises yet I had no idea how I was going to fulfill them. But they sounded nice. And I was black so that would look good for this company since it had a history of discrimination back in the fifties. Do you think I would be respected by the people whom had been in the business for 20 years and had worked hard to one day get the top spot? Those people would respect the position of CEO and would show me respect because it is now the position held by me, if for nothing else to keep their jobs. One of those promises I made to the company when campaigning for the position was free cars for all employees. Well that sounds great right? Unrealistic, but great. But what did I care? I was tired of seeing folks have to take the bus to work and paying for cabs. Now who do you think I am going to hire to help me figure this thing out? Well since I have absolutely no experience I am going to have to choose someone I can trust. I am going to appoint my buddy James to help me pull this off. James managed a Foot Locker back in the day so certainly he can give some insight. In this scenario, can you figure out the main thing I am missing that would have greatly assisted me in figuring this whole thing out?

Well I had never run anything before. And having management experience and executive experience would almost be essential to get everyone on the same page, or at least a meeting somewhere in the middle. Having that experience would also have given me a little insight into what I might do if someone or a certain group of associates thought my plan was admirable, but fiscally impossible. One of the keys to being a good manager or executive is to be able to bring everyone together and get ideas from all sides of the table. Not just the side that agrees with you. You have to remember the people that chose me did so, not because of my experience, but rather what I promised them I could accomplish. If and when I run into some opposition I am not sure I am capable of handling it because I have never run into anything like this on such a large scale. And a company this huge is probably not where I should have started getting "on the job" training. Hell, I can't even remember a time when someone disagreed with me outside of a history class. But it all sounded so good at the time. What have I gotten myself and this company into? I can't run a company this size just because I am cool and I promised people a lot of free stuff. I really wish I had some executive experience now but it is too late.

I want everyone reading this to understand, I am not what some like to call "Obama bashing." I actually think he is a pretty cool person. He seems to be very smart and is the type of person I could learn a lot from. I would like to have a beer with him sometime. He seems like a good family man and I have no doubt his intentions are good. That being said, those intentions are not logical or very well thought out. Unfortunately, it takes more than those good attributes to take on a task as large as running the most powerful country on the planet. I would hope everyone could agree with me on that. That is precisely why I made the statement earlier about Democrats voting with their hearts and

Republicans voting with their heads. That is especially important given the state of affairs the country has been in for past few years. I would give you details but that would take too long. Before Obama, the last few presidents have been governors of a particular state. In my opinion this is a perfect first step in becoming Commander in Chief. Even as governor you are subject to ridicule from the other side. That is what I call "healthy experience." As a matter of fact, 17 of the presidents throughout history were governors. Think of a governor as the president of a particular state and not the country. You deal with similar issues and have similar hurdles that the president has, just on a much smaller scale. Does it always work out for the better? Absolutely not, but you have play the odds. You have to elect whom you deem most qualified. The Office of The President of the United States is a position much too powerful to elect someone just because you like them. There is too much at stake especially in this day and age, where we are not liked by many across the globe. Do you think Vladimir Putin respects Obama because he is cool or because he has a law degree? Open your eyes people while you still have a chance. I feel like I have said that before but I cannot stress it enough.

I would like you to ask yourself one very important question;

When the new health care law was passed, do you think Obama knew 5 million people were going to lose insurance coverage? If you recall he said the exact opposite on multiple occasions. Either way you answer this question, it will lead you to the same unfortunate outcome. I will say this much, I knew it was going to happen with just minimal research. I did not have to read the entire bill. But the Democrats were banking on the fact that no one cared about details. It was just the "right thing to do." And if you were against, it you were a hateful person who does not care about the poor. I have to be perfectly honest with you, I don't make enough money to care about the poor. One day I hope I will make enough money to chip in but until then, I have my own responsibilities such as taking care of my family. And I do donate but I donate what I feel I can. I don't want to donate what someone thinks I should. And to all you wealthy Democrats out there, on your tax form there is a section where you can donate any amount that you would like. I would suggest you do that until I catch up with you financially. And that might be sooner than later if you let me live my life and stay out of the way.

Chapter 9

CRASH ON J BIRD ROAD

The Conclusion

Have you ever tried to do the right thing and it just blows up in your face. That has happened to me a few times in my journey but this one is definitely the worst. I brought J Bird over to Julie's house because I knew he felt defeated. I have felt that way a time or two in my life, but I truly think this was the first time he ever felt that. Him losing his job, and the way he lost it, was unable to be fixed. The grandparents could not fix it and neither could money. What was done was done and I knew that put him in a fragile state. That is why I chose to do something for him totally outside of the box. I thought by taking him to see Julie not only would it lift his spirits, but I was kind of hoping they could relate to each other. Julie had lost everything and was slowly getting it all back and J Bird felt like he lost everything in his own weird sort of way. It turned out to be a bad idea getting them together that night. It turned out to be a horrible idea.

I had not heard from the Birdman in a couple of days so I decided to stop by his house one day after work. When I got there, he was gone but his grandparents were there. "Hey Mrs. Shaw, do you know when J Bird is going to be home?" I asked. "I am really not sure," She responded. "He and Julie are supposed to be going out to eat. She is such a sweet girl." "Ok" I responded. "Just tell him I stopped by." When I got back in my car I sat there for a second stunned. I thought to myself, "What the hell have I just done?" Here we have a recovering drug addict hanging out with a drug addict that is not in recovery. We also have a grown woman who is hanging out with J Bird who is the most psychologically challenged person I know. This is a disaster waiting to happen. I did not mind them hanging out at all but not by themselves, never by themselves. She could potentially destroy him. Julie was a good person but she was from the streets. She knew how to hustle with the best of them. And J Bird lived in a fantasy world. I did not have to go looking for them as they came by my house later that evening…together. They both looked so happy. J Bird had taken her to Outback and they went to a movie. I did not want to ruin their moment so I just asked about the movie and what they had to eat. I knew deep down these 2 unstable individuals did not need to be hanging around together unsupervised. "So what are you guys getting into after this?" I asked. "Well I am taking her home and I am probably heading to the house." "You wanna come crash at my place tonight?" J Bird asked. "Thanks J Bird, but I was just getting ready to go to bed," I replied. Even though I knew I was not going to get much sleep that night. "Ok man well we will see you later," J Bird said. And off they went, two crazies into the night. I knew Julie's agenda. And she knew J Bird. You see Julie was never a bad person. She tried to be a good parent to my niece and nephews but the drugs just consumed her. My brother put up with it for way longer than the family wanted him too but eventually he realized the kids were in danger. That is when he decided to leave. Julie knew J Bird had money. She knew all about his grandparents and had met them on many occasions. She also knew J Bird liked her and would give her anything she wanted. I was going to have to handle this with kid gloves for sure. I could not believe these two were hanging out and I was the one that started it. I am such a genius some times. Low and behold, the same evening the two of them left my house, J Bird showed back up about two hours later. I had a feeling he would actually. I knew he would not be able to contain his excitement just sitting at home. That is why he asked if I wanted to come with him earlier. And that is why I told him no. I would rather him tell me here at my place so I could sleep in my own bed afterwards and not a couch. The first words out of my mouth when he came in and we sat down were, "Be careful." There was no sense in beating around the bush on this one. And he responded exactly like I thought he would. "You would not believe the fun we had tonight," J Bird said, completely ignoring my words of caution. "I just want you to be careful J Bird that is all," I said. "Julie is a grown woman with three kids who is divorced and has a lot on her plate. Do you really think you can handle all of that? Not to mention her previous addiction?"

I continued. J Bird never really had a girl friend and frankly I did not want Julie to be his first. And I knew she did not care about him nearly as much as he thought she did. I am sure she liked hanging out with him, but the look on his face showed something way more serious. "I just don't want you to get hurt that is all." I told him. "You are not jealous are you?" J Bird asked. I guess I should have seen that one coming. In a way I guess I did sound like I was trying to end it before it began. And he clearly did not see the reason why. "No Birdman, I am not jealous," I said. "She was my sister for like 8 years or something." J Bird did not get what I was saying. He was already too taken in by her and I set the whole thing up.

There was not much else I could do in regards to Birdman's situation. We found out a few days later that Julie was dating someone else. J Bird did not even care. As long as she made time for him he was ok with that. Their relationship lasted for about a month. I got to see Julie way more than expected within that time period. At least once a week they would either come by the house or I would see her at J Bird's home. I loved Julie because she was a part of my life for a long time and she was the mother of my niece and nephews. But she was crazy and so was J Bird. Two crazy people do not need to be in a relationship. Someone, either the guy or the girl, needs to have some sanity to balance each other out. I guess that is just my opinion. I would actually talk to Julie on the phone some times. She would call me to see if I had seen the Birdman on occasion. She would even come by unannounced at times. I guess she thought things were ok between her and I. I guess she thought we were cool. I played along for a while but I really did not want her back in my life like that. Her and my brother's relationship was extremely volatile at times and seeing her just brought back some of those memories I would rather not rehash. The conversations we had were totally different than the conversation I had with J Bird. She would tell me one day that she and J Bird were just having fun and the next day J Bird would tell me he was thinking about asking her if they could get a place together. They were completely on different pages and that is what ultimately ended their little "fling." Julie called me one day not soon after J Bird had mentioned the whole plan about the apartment. "Hey you!" She said when I answered. "What's up Julie?" I responded. "I think I am going to need to call things off with the Birdman. He is getting way too attached," Julie says to me. "No kidding," I said to myself. "Julie, you have known J Bird for a long time and you know how attached he can get. Did you not think this was going to happen? Or did you just not think?" I replied. "Well he knows I have a boyfriend," Julie then said. "J Bird does not care," I responded. "I am guessing he is thinking when y'all move in together you will leave your boyfriend but that is not going to happen is it?" I said. "Move in together?" Julie said quite surprised. I guess J Bird had not told her about that plan but I was just done by this time. "You know if you break it off with him, he is going to be destroyed right?" I said. "I know, that is why I was kind of hoping you could tell him for me. You could break it to him better than I could," Julie said. That was the reason she called me. That same old Julie, some things never change. Now you are probably thinking I was going to say no and hang up the phone. But I did not do that. Maybe it would be better coming from me as I had no idea how he would react. I would, however, rather me get the reaction than her. So I told her I would do it. I told her I would do it today because if I did not this charade would just continue until she just started avoiding him, thus driving him even more crazy. "I will tell him Julie but you have to do me a favor." I said. "Anything!" Julie said desperately. "I don't want you to talk to him anymore. If I tell him today you can't give him hope that there is a chance by continuing to stay in contact with him. Can you do that?" I asked. And of course she promptly replied, "Absolutely!" She just wanted it over. She had used him enough and the fun was now over. And once again I am the one stuck picking up the pieces. I caused this one though, so I had no one to blame but myself.

I guess it was about seven in the evening when I drove over to J Bird's place. Mr. Shaw was on the porch as usual and said his routine, "Hey buddy!" as I walked inside. I don't even know if I responded back. J Bird was in the kitchen with his grandmother. When J Bird saw me he gave the usual response, "Hey buddy" just like his grandfather. I always found that so amusing, but not tonight. "Hey Birdman you wanna go for a drive?" I asked. "Ok but only if I can drive?" He responded. J Bird always wanted to drive. And I never argued with him because he did, after all, have the nicer car by a long shot. "No problem here man. You can drive if you want." I said. We left the house about 10 minutes later. I hopped in the passenger seat, J Bird cranked the car and we were off.

J Bird had been coddled and protected his whole life and I had been one of those enablers that I speak of in earlier chapters. No, I was not afraid to tell him what was right and wrong. But watching him take multiple turns for the worse, and me not being more firm with him, was not the right thing to do. I should have spoken more loudly. I could have. But I understood who he was and was probably always going to be. Remember when I said "Never take advice from anyone that does not have what you want?" Well I did not have anything J Bird wanted. He had everything and that was his main issue. He had everything except the ability to rationally think. He never had too for so many years and old habits and tendencies are hard to break. I know that all too well. I knew what I had to do. And I was just going to come out and say it. If I did not just come out and say it, I would just be prolonging the inevitable. "So where are we headed?" J Bird asked. "Let's just hit the highway. I just need to talk to you for a minute." I responded. He seemed so happy and I was about to crush him. I would rather it be me than her though. "J Bird we have a problem." I started. "I spoke with Julie today. And we had a long conversation about you guy's relationship." I said. "I haven't spoken to her since yesterday but I did leave her a message. Is she ok?" J Bird said. "She is fine Birdman but I think you guys are on two separate pages with this whole relationship thing." I continued. "She called me earlier to tell me she did not think things were going to work out between you two. She asked me to tell you she thinks you guys need to stop hanging out. I am sorry dude." I finished. Then silence came over the car. It was an eerie silence. I just waited for him to speak as I really did not have anything else to say. J Bird did not speak. All I remember is a tear going down his cheek slowly and the car picking up speed at a rapid pace. J Bird sped up and got right up on the vehicle in front of us' bumper. He then quickly changed lanes and sped ahead of the car, pulling in front of it. Once he was in front of the car he slammed on his brakes, not enough to where they locked up, but enough to where the car behind us came within inches of slamming into us. "Birdman what the hell are you doing!!!" I exclaimed. But he did not say a word. Once the vehicle behind us slowed down J Bird slowed down with it to match speeds. I do not remember what kind of vehicle it was but it was no Maxima. J Bird knew that vehicle could not out run his car. The vehicle attempted to speed up and pass J Bird. By then I think they knew he was crazy and they were in danger, but J Bird just sped up again, passing them. For the second time, he pulled in front of them and slammed on the brakes causing the car, now behind us, to do the same once more. "Dude chill out, you are going to kill someone!" I shouted at him once again. His face just stayed looking straight ahead and I knew at that time he had finally lost it. This time it was for real. I did not know how this was going to end but it was not looking good. And I am sure the other vehicle was terrified by now. I could not even tell who was in the car as it was dark. All I could tell was it was multiple people. I took my only chance to get out of the vehicle when J Bird pulled over on the shoulder to wait for the car to catch up. This last time he passed them they stopped and started going very slow. I guess they were hoping he would just keep driving. I don't even remember if he came to a complete stop. All I remember is jumping out of the car and him taking off again right as I hit the ground. He could have killed me. He continued driving down the highway and I just stood there watching his car get smaller and smaller in the distance. I was stunned to say the least. I knew I was a long way from home but I decided to start walking.

I needed that walk to clear my head after what I had just experienced. I thought to myself "Maybe I should have just let Julie tell him." Anyways, I think I had walked about 2 miles when who shows up? J Bird of course. He pulls back up on the shoulder and apologized. "I am sorry man I just lost it." Please get back in the car." He said. Now I feel like a girl on a bad date wow! I figured since I had a long way to go, and I was tired what the heck. "Take me home please Birdman." I said. I did not look at him and he did not say another word. I did not even ask him what happened after I jumped out of the car. I just wanted to go home. J Bird dropped me off at my house. I went in and laid down hoping that night was over. Of course it was not.

"Hello." I answered the phone half asleep. "Hey buddy its J Bird. I was wondering if you could come over tonight because I am really going through some things right now." J Bird said on the phone. "Seriously, J Bird? I am half asleep and am not coming over tonight man," I said. "You just need to get some sleep." That guy asked me at least 10 times on that one fall call to please come over. One thing I forgot to mention about J Bird is he was very persistent. So much so, that it drove me crazy. You could tell in all of his years he had not been told no very many times. Eventually I just had to tell him I was going back to bed and hung up the phone. I knew this was serious but I was done. I also knew that he was about done. J Bird had reached the end of his rope and the news I gave him earlier that night might have finished him off. I knew that is why he wanted me to come over. I knew he was desperate. He would not have called me, after what he did that night on the highway, unless he had no other choice. But I just could no longer do it. Having him as a friend was so taxing on one's mind. I did not know what he was going to do that night and frankly I did not care. I even thought he may go so far as to kill himself. I actually thought to myself, for a split second, that it may not have been a bad idea. J Bird was gone anyways and I saw it that evening in the car. And there was nothing else I could do to fix him.

I don't remember the score of the game or even who won. But I do remember that day. A couple of friends and I were over at my brothers place watching the Alabama Tennessee football game. Back then it was actually a rivalry (Sorry I just had to put that in there). 9 times out of 10 we always gathered for important games at my brother place. We were having a good time drinking some cold ones when I got a call. At the time I was outside by myself smoking a cigarette being harassed by a cop for having an open beer on my bothers porch. I mean seriously did he not have anything better to do? Maybe he was just pissed that he could not watch the game, who knows. I answered the phone and it was J Bird. I had not spoken to him in a couple of weeks. I did not even know if he was still alive. "Hey buddy, it's me." He said in a very faint voice. "What's up dude?" My usual greeting. "I just called to tell you I love you and you have always been my best friend. I have been shot and the police have my mom's house surrounded." J Bird said. "I don't think I am going to make it out of this one." Ok so if you heard something like that you probably would be stunned and surprised. Well given the fact that this was J Bird, and the fact that I had a few beers, I thought he was just trying to get attention again.

I thought he wanted me to come over and this was an elaborate excuse. A good one I might add but I still did not believe him totally. I will say in the back of my mind I thought there could have been a little truth to it but not exactly what he was saying. Maybe he went off on his mom and she called the cops on him or something. And I wasn't going anywhere at that point in time. It is funny how you can remember so much about a specific event in your life but some of the most significant things escape you. I honestly have no idea how I responded to him when he said what he said. And whatever it was I said could not have been memorable. But I do remember finishing the game. It was almost like that conversation did not even happen. Most of it escapes me.

I went on about my life for a good week not even thinking about the Birdman. The last few weeks had actually been great. There was no drama whatsoever. It wasn't until a few days later that I even thought about J Bird and that weird conversation. I decided to call him and see what was up.

"Hey Mrs. Shaw, is J Bird there?" I asked. "You haven't heard?" Mrs. Shaw asked. "He is jail downtown." Ok so he was not kidding when we last spoke on the phone. I had to pretend I did not know anything to get the full details. Clearly Mrs. Shaw did not know J Bird had called me that day. Mrs. Shaw began to tell me the story and I will paraphrase it for you: J Bird was at his mom's the day he called me. His drug buddy, whom I had not seen in a while, was over there with him. Mrs. Shaw was not sure what J Bird had taken but it sent him into a rage. So much so, that his friend left the house in a hurry. J Bird's mother was home at the time and she was the one that told Mrs. Shaw the story. She told her that J Bird had threatened her when she told him he had to go. I guess he was really going crazy for his mom to try and get him to leave. He then went into the kitchen and grabbed a knife and pointed it at her. That sent his mother running into her room and locking the door. She then called the police. When the police arrived she somehow made it out of the back door without J Bird noticing and then ran around to the front where the police were. She explained to them that her son was in the house going crazy and that he had a knife. Please remember I was not there and I am strictly going off of second hand information. One thing I have not mentioned in this entire story was J Bird's love for weapons (Yes weapons of all things). One of his favorite was an SKS rifle he used to love shooting in his backyard. There was an old storage shed he used to love shooting at. I never shot it but remembered how loud that thing use to be. Come to find out, he had that rifle at his mom's house when all of this occurred. Maybe it had been there a while, maybe not but I had not seen it or heard him talk about it in forever. While the police were standing outside talking to J Bird's mom, he opened up one of the front windows and started firing away. From what I was told he started shooting at the 2 police cars that were parked out front. I tend to believe that because if he wanted to shoot them he could have easily. The front yard was not very large at all. Needless to say what started as a domestic dispute had turned into a standoff. The entire police force of that town was called to the house. J Bird's mom lived on the outskirts of town so that was not a whole lot of people. The streets were blocked off for blocks and the police did not move in as they had no idea where in the house he was. From what

I hear no one moved until the SWAT team arrived. By then, Birdman's grandparents were already on the scene pleading with police to let them talk to him but it was too late for that. The SWAT team carefully walked up to the house, body armor and all, and managed to get J Bird to surrender after the tear gas was thrown into the house.

I sat there on the phone speechless. "We are going to go see him at the jail tomorrow evening if you would like to come?" Mrs. Shaw asked. It sounded like she was inviting me to dinner. Always the optimist, that Mrs. Shaw was. I told Mrs. Shaw I would go with them and hung up the phone. I would call back for the details later.

At that point in time a lot of different feelings went through my head. The first thing I realized was that he was telling the truth the last time I spoke to him. The second thing was I had never been to visit someone in jail. I mean this was the jail downtown. The rest of that day is kind of a blur. I am pretty sure I went to work as usual but I assure you my head was not in it that day. I was going to see J Bird this evening with his grandparents. I remember going to the jail that evening. I met the both of them there after work. I remember seeing Mr. Shaw and he looked like he had been crying. Mrs. Shaw looked just the same as she always did. But you could tell neither of them had slept well since all of this happened. I was the first one to go up and see him. It was just like the movies but I had no idea the glass was going to be that thick. It was like 4 times the thickness of normal bullet proof glass. I talked with J Bird for about 5 minutes. It was very emotional and sad seeing him in there. He told me that he shot himself and I saw the wound in his right shoulder. I thought to myself, that was a weird place to shoot yourself. Mrs. Shaw told me later she thought the cops did it, not J Bird. He told me they were trying to charge him with 4 counts of attempted murder and his bail was 2 million dollars. I don't think the Shaw's had ten percent of that just sitting around. That entire experience was very surreal.

The one thing that stood out the most about that whole evening was not that J Bird was in prison. I kind of saw that coming in a sad sort of way. I could tell his grandfather was crushed. Mr. Shaw never said much but when it was his turn to talk to J Bird I heard him start crying as I walked out the door. I heard him right before the door shut behind me. At that point I felt bad about anything I ever said to him regarding J Bird's downward spiral. I felt bad because I was right. I felt bad because Mr. Shaw knew I was right.

Well this sad story is finally coming to an end. J Bird's grandfather was a retired police officer and was able to use some connections to get the bail down to two hundred thousand dollars. I guess they determined he was not shooting at the cops but just at the cop cars. I am not sure really. J Bird made bail and when I saw him the first thing I said to him was "Dude you have gotten fat?" I thought jail would do the opposite to one's body. He was not a muscular build but an "I eat too much" build. I knew he had gotten out because his grandfather told me the day before. He showed up at my house and I have to say it was good seeing him. But he and I both knew things would never be the same. I saw him a few times after that but knowing he was going to prison hit him hard. He realized he was no longer invincible. I think that hit him even harder.

I don't even remember the last time I saw or spoke to the Birdman. I don't remember the last time I saw his grandparents. I don't even know if they are still alive. I know the trial was eventually held after months of the date being pushed back. I do not know what the exact outcome was though. I know he went to prison and is still in prison to this day and that was years ago. Every few months I Google his name and I can see what prison he is in and his release date. I know it is him because his birthday was on May 28. That is the same day as my sisters and we would sometime celebrate them at the same time.

So now you know who J Bird was to me. You also now know who J Bird was to himself. I hope the story has been interesting and enlightening. I know it was to me because I lived it. Did I fail the Birdman? Did I enable him? In all honesty I think I did. I use to tell friends of mine that a lot of what happened was my fault. I was the first person he ever drank with. I was the first person he ever smoked pot with. I opened him up to a world that he not only was not ready for, but given his personality never ever needed to venture into. I had to be convinced by others that it was not my fault. J Bird was a grown man at this point in time. I still wonder, to this day, if there was any possible way the Shaws would have been able to hide J Bird in that paradise forever. Could he have been the "boy who never grew up," like Peter Pan? Well to answer that, I realized it was quite simply, no. And the reason was his grandparents were not going to be everlasting like a fairytale. I think deep down they realized that also but would never utter that sentiment out loud. I think they were looking for someone to show him the real world in small increments until he was ready. The world and people do not work that way and that was their mistake thinking it did. They assumed I could live my real life and keep him sheltered out there in it at the same time. But that is too much to assume from anyone, especially from someone like me. I was trying to find myself at the same time. Do the Shaws hate me? I don't think they could ever hate anyone. Does J Bird hate me? I can't answer that question. All I know is I was the only real friend he ever had.

That is why he saved, what he thought, was his last phone call for me.

Chapter 10

TO THE REPUBLICANS...FOR WHICH THEY STAND

I do not think there was any exact time that I realized I was a Republican. I will say this, the final events that occurred with the Birdman and the conversation I had with Kate were within the same couple of months. The reason I know that for sure is because the apartment I was watching that game at, when I received that call, was my brothers. And he only lived there for a few months before remarrying and purchasing a home. I also know I was a supervisor at that tech call center during my brother's brief apartment stay. It is really funny when you put your life's story on paper some dates and times do become clearer. Not exact dates and times, but close enough. I just now realized that was the time in my life I actually found something that worked for me. And I figured it out on my own. And it still works to this day. I made it. And it was not impossible.

It was not even complicated. I am not saying that was when I became a Republican, but that is when I saw, in a very short amount of time, what dependency can do to people. And I knew the Republicans were not about that. I live in a city full of Democrats and saw the alternative. Needless to say, what I had just experienced personally, I did not like.

Now I am not a religious person. That is not to say I do not believe in god, because I do. I just don't believe everyone that does not believe exactly what I believe is going to burn in hell. That is just too deep for me. And I also do not believe a person on death row is going to Heaven just because he accepted Christ on his death bed. I frankly would rather a kind hearted atheist, than a mass murderer any day of the week to spend all of eternity with. I keep my politics here on earth and not in the afterlife. And if my beliefs aren't good enough to get me through those pearly gates, it is probably somewhere I would not want to be anyway. If taking care of my family and working hard isn't enough, then so be it. I also do not disagree with gay marriage. Frankly, I don't think government should have any place in marriage. That is something, I think, should be left up to you, your partner and your maker. I feel abortion is wrong but it is legal. And for you extreme conservatives out there I have news for you, "It is always going to be legal." I am also a very private person. I have never been on Facebook, Twitter or anything like that. I use a computer at work, but the one at home is rarely used. If I am researching a topic or looking for a movie time, then it is the computer to the rescue. I keep to myself and my family most of the time, when I am not at work. You may say thirty eight is not old but I beg to differ.

I have seen and experienced many things and most of them are not in this book. My soul is old and my conscience is tired.

I go to church every Sunday but it is not to hear the word. It is because I work there as the sound technician. I don't really get into the sermons but it always makes me feel good when I see others enjoy them. I don't think the government, Democrat or Republican, truly has a clue as to what to do with my tax dollars. That is why I affiliate myself with the party that wants to take the least. Charles Barkley made a statement once talking about rookie athletes and their new found wealth. He talked about never giving any money to help someone start a business because that business would fail. Why would it fail, you ask? It was not their money to begin with. They did not work for it and therefore the risk is minimized. The risk is less "real." And the smaller the risk, the less driven you are going to be to ensure your business' success. He is right. I look at my tax dollars that way. The government just takes it before I even see my paycheck. They did not work for it and that is why they throw it around like there is an unlimited supply. I bet they don't do that with the money they earn. What do you think? I look on TV at all of these ads of politicians and you know what? None of them relate to me. None of them look like me. I don't have the picture perfect family. I don't wear suits and ties. I am not a hard core Christian. I am not a Conservative. What I am is a person that does not look like you but can relate to you on issues that are important to me. You should do the same. I can relate to Republican beliefs much more so than Democrat beliefs. Not all, but enough.

Our party needs more people like me. We are losing for a reason. And the only reason we may win the next race is because of the god awful job of the Democrats. The Democrats screwing this place up so bad should not be the only reason we should win. I don't like being the lesser of two evils. And there are many just like me. I guess we could be called "Unlikely Allies." Even though I voted for Romney, it was probably a good bit of "Unlikely Allies" that did not and therefore we lost. Conservative Republicans are out of touch with us. And don't tell me you guys think for one second any of us can relate to Mitt Romney. He seems like a great guy and definitely had the credentials, but you also have to be relatable to the normal American, the one you don't see in Washington. That is why we lost. We did not lose the second election because Barack Obama got more votes. We lost because less of us voted. I know plenty of Republicans just like me. Even if they do not associate themselves with a party, I know plenty of them that feel the same as me. But I also know there are more uninformed voters who are Democrats than there are "Unlikely Allies." We can take a large chunk of that crowd, along with those that are neither Democrat nor Republican. But we have to be able to relate to them. The crazy thing is we do relate to them. They are people just like us who go to work every day to provide for their families. You see them at work. You see them at church and in the stores. When uninformed people think Republican they think "white." They think "rich." They think "Anti women." And most importantly they think "anti minority." That is how we are portrayed by the left and frankly, if the uninformed stay that way, it will never change. I for one am not sexist, racist, rich or white. I am a strong, well informed, black man who pays attention to what is going on around me. I love rap music and love listening to it LOUD. As far as music is concerned rap is all I listen too. I find it very entertaining and that is what it is there for, entertainment. And I have seen more than most. But in the end I am still just a normal guy with an interesting story to tell. Keep the message simple and relatable to ordinary folk like myself. My politics may not be ordinary but believe me when I say I am. The world is changing and we as a party need to change with it or get "left" behind.

Chapter 11

MY TWO CENTS

We have reached the end of this book and I sincerely hope you have been entertained and enlightened, but most of all I hope you have been empowered. I have tried to give you examples that stress the importance of family, friendship and focus. I have tried not to make this book all about politics, but I cannot stress enough the importance of knowledge and research. A college degree is not required to go to the library or surf the web. Do your own research and decide what is best for you and your family. The decisions I have made throughout my journey have shaped who I am as a person. A lot of things that transpired in my life have made things easier. A lot more of the things I have done in my life have made things harder. In the end, however, I would not be the person I am today had those situations not have come into my life. Those situations have made me well....ME. I waited until the end of this book to give you a question to ask yourself. I would like for you to ask yourself the following:

Besides the question, "Is this guys crazy?" Who do you think this book is truly meant for?

(Hint) It is probably not for the person who bought it and read it first. You already get it.

The crazy part is absolutely correct so I don't want you to spend too much time with that. I am crazy about my family. I am crazy about my country. I am crazy about my future and what things will look like when all of my children, nieces and nephews are grown. And yes, in the grand scheme of things I am just crazy.

Before I finally wrap this up into a nice little package, I need to explain to you why I have written this book in the first place. It is actually for a couple of reasons. Reason number one is the easiest to explain so I will start with it. We have some extremely important elections coming up this November and if we do not take control back in the Senate, I fear the worst. If you think things are going along just fine right now, I honestly hope you do not vote. Voting is a right and not a privilege. Take it seriously or do not take it at all.

Secondly, I have had an interesting life and a story I thought you would find interesting. As interesting as the story has been, my lifestyle in my younger years has taken its toll on me. I am 38 years of age but I feel like I am 48. And my body feels like it is 58. Don't take my word for it, just ask it. I was diagnosed with a debilitating disease a few years back. I am not exactly sure if it has anything to do with my lifestyle, but I am sure that did not help me from not getting it. I will not tell you what I have as that is not the point I am trying to make. Just know that it is not contagious and it is not going to ultimately kill me. I will have plenty of time for something else to do that. But what this disease is doing is slowly taking away my eyesight. When I have what I call an "attack," I lose a good portion of my sight. I go to my neurologist and he prescribes me some steroids. A couple of days after taking them my vision returns but it never comes back %100. I have not had an "attack" in the last two or three years so this is not something that happens all the time. The problem is, it could happen again tomorrow or it could never happen again. That uncertainty, I have learned to live with. But if and when it does happen again, this computer screen I am typing on now will probably not be big enough for me to continue. I am at a point now with this disease where I am truly struggling to do my job. I hide it quite well but I will not be able to hide it forever. Only one person in this entire company even knows I have what I have. In coming to the realization that my "hustle" will eventually come to an end, as all good things do, I have gotten into real estate investing. It is a lot of fun, there is great money to be made and I can do it part time. Not to mention a house is much easier to see than words on a computer monitor. Homes are a little bit bigger than most fonts I have noticed.

Always remember, your actions will never change until your thinking does. If you are trying to save people with other's money, vote Democrat. If you are trying to save and make money all the while empowering others to do the same, vote Republican. There is not enough money in the world to change the way anyone thinks. If you took all of the rich people's money and gave it to a Democrat politician, nothing in society would change. Those Democrats would keep the poor person just that… poor. Granted a poor person would garner a nicer place to stay and maybe a free cell phone, but they would still think like a poor person. And in turn so will their children most of the time. We see it every day. You don't have to take my word for it just look around your poorest areas. These places are goldmines for Democrats. You should see the houses these politicians get out of the deal. Now I am not saying all Democrats are in it for themselves, just as I am not saying all Republicans are not crooks. Anytime you hold a position that gives you power to vote yourself a pay raise, there is going to be bad apples a plenty on both sides. As a matter of fact, I don't think I, personally, could handle that kind of power but that is just me being real. If you haven't noticed yet, I have a very opportunistic personality. But you have heard my story already. Politicians are a necessity in our society and you need to take the side of the one that can relate more to you and your family's needs. Simply do the research and use your head. Think for yourself and have no one in your ear telling you they know better (I have said that before). The biggest sellouts and racists are the ones that think you can't do it yourself and are not capable of learning. They get paid real money to keep you in that mind set. After all, do you think they would assist you for free? Just ask Jesse and Al. They make a living off of the color of your skin. They feed their families off of ignorance.

Get pissed, get over it and then get a grip. If you get offended the Dems will be by your side in a New York minute…for a price of course.

I am going to be as blunt and as honest as I can be right now in closing. This book is not for everyone and was not written for everyone. But if you have made it this far the answers to the question above and the questions to follow should become clearer. And there is not a wrong answer to any of them (even though I will give you my two cents). Remember, you are asking only yourself and you're the only one listening. Once again thank you for your time and patience. And no, there will not be another book from me, about me, as I have nothing else to tell.

I think we can all agree that is a very, very good thing.

The End

QUESTIONS
TO PONDER

1. Are you a Democrat and you voted for Barrack Obama strictly because he is black?
2. Are you a Republic and you did not vote for Barrack Obama strictly because he is black?

My Two cents: If you answered yes to either of the above 2 questions, please sit the book down and slowly walk away. You have way bigger problems than this book can solve. But I do thank you for reading.

3. **Are you a Democrat strictly because you are black?**
4. **Are you a Republican strictly because you are white?**

My two cents: If you answered yes to either of the above 2 questions, you are severely hampering your development as an individual. You are classifying yourself as a color and that greatly limits your

options. You can identify with a color without it identifying you. Just be careful with this one as it is very tricky.

Opportunity lets you put your foot inside the door of success, but it doesn't break the door down for you.

Opportunities are not windfalls. Winning a sweepstakes makes you instantly rich; encountering an opportunity means you will have to go to work. When you have attuned your mind to recognize opportunities, you will understand that most often they involve the exploitation of some potential, such as providing a new or better service, streamlining production, or reaching a new market. This is why the habit of initiative is so important. You must be prepared to act as soon as you recognize an opportunity. The action may be simply further investigation, or it may be making an instant sale. Most often, however, an opportunity takes time and perseverance to develop.

~Napoleon Hill~